KU-166-482

BEST-EVER GRILLS

Consultant Editor:
Valerie Ferguson

LORENZ BOOKS

Contents

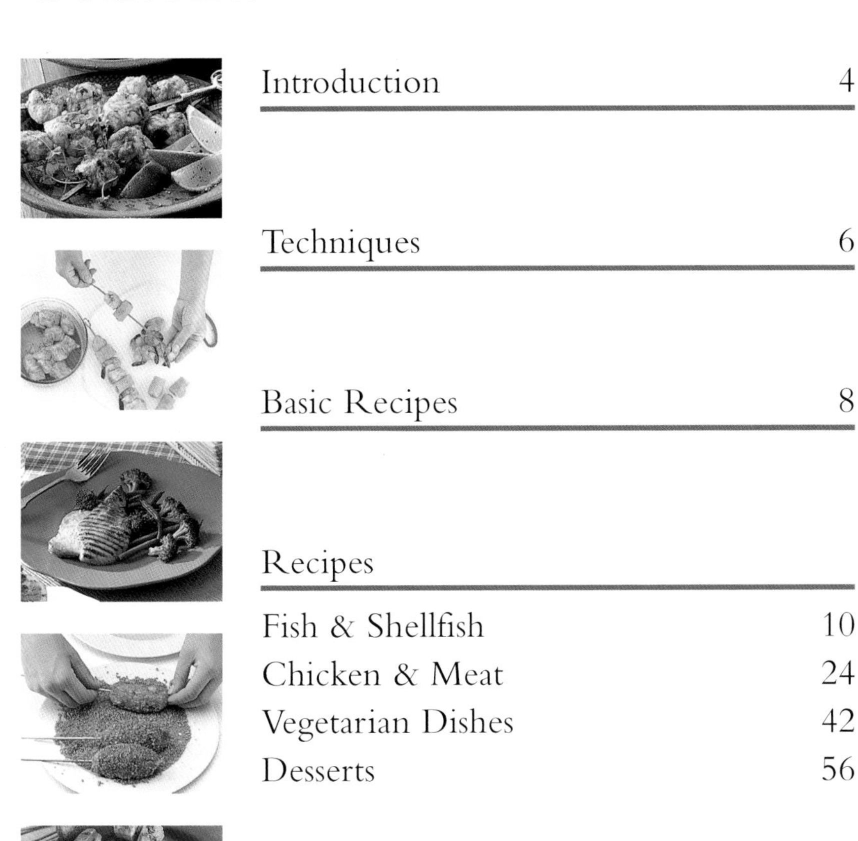

Introduction

The joy of grilling food is that it is so quick and easy – perfect for the busy life we lead today. Many types of food can be cooked in this way – fish, poultry, meat, vegetables and fruit – but it must be of the best quality and, in the case of meat, the tenderest cuts.

Grilling subjects food to intense direct heat, which can be drying; marinating it beforehand avoids this problem and also opens up the possibility of a wide range of delicious flavourings. Of course, marinating adds to the preparation time, but it just requires a little advance organization, and once the marinating is done the actual cooking is still quick.

Simply grilled food, brushed with just a small amount of oil or low fat marinade, is also a healthy option for people who are watching the fat content of their diet.

Whatever your tastes, this collection of recipes offers new, unusual ideas for your grill as well as the traditional favourites. There is something for everyone: spicy and exotic grills with fish, poultry and meat, and luscious desserts for the sweet-toothed. There is a whole chapter of simple, tasty vegetarian dishes too.

Most of the recipes in this book are also suitable for barbecuing – the great outdoor version of grilling.

Marinating

Marinades are used to add flavour, moisten or tenderize foods, particularly meat, and are especially useful for food that is to be grilled. Marinades can be either savoury or sweet and are as varied as you wish: spicy, fruity, fragrant or exotic. Certain classic combinations always work well. Usually, it's best to choose oily marinades for dry foods, such as lean meat or white fish, and wine- or vinegar-based marinades for rich foods with a higher fat content. Most marinades don't contain salt, which can draw out the juices from meat; it's best to add salt just before cooking. About 150 ml/¼ pint/⅔ cup is enough for approximately 500 g/1¼ lb food.

1 Place the food for marinating in a wide dish or bowl, preferably large enough to allow it to lie in a single layer.

2 Mix together thoroughly the ingredients for the marinade.

3 Pour the marinade over the food and turn the food to coat it evenly.

4 Cover the dish and refrigerate from 30 minutes up to several hours, depending on the recipe, turning the food over occasionally and spooning the marinade over it.

5 Remove the food with a slotted spoon, or lift it out with tongs, and drain off and reserve the marinade. If necessary, allow the food to come to room temperature before cooking.

6 Use the marinade for basting or brushing the food during cooking.

Grilling

Preheat the grill thoroughly and grease the grill pan. Bring food to room temperature, do not overcook, and serve immediately.

FISH:

1 The intense, dry heat of grilling is best used for fish with a lot of natural oil, such as salmon, mackerel and tuna. Ensure that the fish is 8–10 cm/3–4 in away from the heat source and turn if the recipe specifies.

2 Leaner fish can also be grilled – baste it frequently to keep it moist or cook it in a little liquid. Brush with butter, oil or a basting mixture, according to the recipe, and grill without turning.

POULTRY:

1 Pieces of fairly even thickness, such as chicken breasts and thighs, are best for grilling. Brush with oil, melted butter or as specified.

2 Place the pieces 10–15 cm/4–6 in from the heat source (nearer if less than 2.5 cm/1 in thick). If they brown too quickly, reduce the heat slightly.

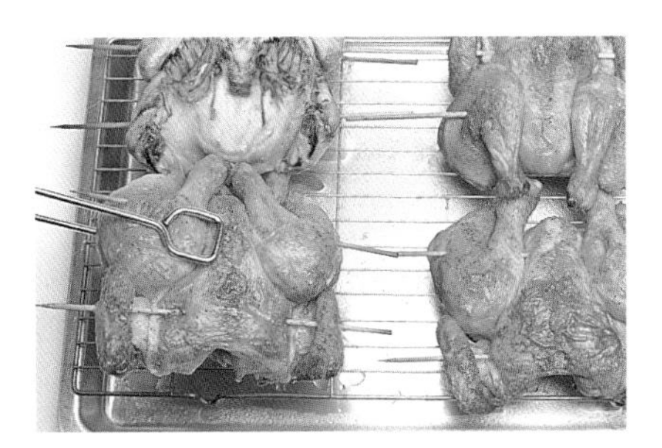

3 Allow 30–35 minutes for a poussin or chicken breast, drumstick or thigh; 10–12 minutes for a skinless, boneless chicken or duck breast. Turn half-way through cooking.

MEAT:

1 Because grilling is a dry-heat cooking method, it suits naturally tender cuts of beef, lamb and pork. These should ideally be no more than 5 cm/2 in thick. Brush with butter, oil or basting sauce, as specified.

2 Place the meat 8 cm/3 in from the heat. Turn during cooking.

Marinades

By using a wide variety of ingredients to achieve different flavours, marinades can transform your grilled food.

BASIC MARINADE
This can be used for meat or fish.

1 garlic clove, crushed
45 ml/3 tbsp sunflower or olive oil
45 ml/3 tbsp dry sherry
15 ml/1 tbsp Worcestershire sauce
15 ml/1 tbsp dark soy sauce
freshly ground black pepper

HERB MARINADE
Good for fish, meat or poultry.

120 ml/4 fl oz/½ cup dry white wine
60 ml/4 tbsp olive oil
15 ml/1 tbsp lemon juice
30 ml/2 tbsp finely chopped fresh herbs, such as parsley, thyme, chives or basil
freshly ground black pepper

HONEY CITRUS MARINADE
Delicious with fish or chicken.

finely grated rind and juice of ½ lime, ½ lemon and ½ small orange
45 ml/3 tbsp sunflower oil
30 ml/2 tbsp clear honey
15 ml/1 tbsp soy sauce
5 ml/1 tsp Dijon mustard
freshly ground black pepper

YOGURT SPICE MARINADE
For fish, meat or poultry.

150 ml/¼ pint/⅔ cup plain yogurt
1 small onion, finely chopped
1 garlic clove, crushed
5 ml/1 tsp finely chopped fresh root ginger
5 ml/1 tsp ground coriander
5 ml/1 tsp ground cumin
2.5 ml/½ tsp ground turmeric

RED WINE MARINADE
Good with red meats and game.

150 ml/¼ pint/⅔ cup dry red wine
15 ml/1 tbsp olive oil
15 ml/1 tbsp red wine vinegar
2 garlic cloves, crushed
2 dried bay leaves, crumbled
freshly ground black pepper

Relishes

These relishes are very easy and quick to prepare and will liven up sausages, burgers and steaks.

QUICK RELISH

Making use of storecupboard ingredients, this quick relish is ideal for an impromptu barbecue. It has a slightly tangy flavour.

45 ml/3 tbsp sweet pickle
15 ml/1 tbsp Worcestershire sauce
30 ml/2 tbsp tomato ketchup
10 ml/2 tsp prepared mustard
15 ml/1 tbsp cider vinegar
30 ml/2 tbsp brown sauce

1 Mix together the sweet pickle, Worcestershire sauce, tomato ketchup and prepared mustard in a bowl, stirring well.

2 Add the cider vinegar and the brown sauce to the mixture and stir thoroughly to combine. Cover the bowl and place the relish in the fridge to chill until required.

CUCUMBER RELISH

A cool, refreshing relish, this may also be used as an excellent dip to serve with crudités as a starter.

½ cucumber
2 celery sticks, chopped
1 green pepper, seeded and chopped
1 garlic clove, crushed
300 ml/½ pint/1¼ cups plain yogurt
15 ml/1 tbsp chopped fresh coriander
freshly ground black pepper

1 Dice the cucumber and place the pieces in a large bowl. Add the chopped celery and green pepper and the crushed garlic.

2 Stir in the plain yogurt and the chopped fresh coriander. Season with freshly ground black pepper. Cover the bowl and chill. Use the relish the same day.

Teriyaki Trout

Marinating trout fillets in this Japanese-inspired teriyaki sauce makes them wonderfully tender and tasty.

Serves 4

INGREDIENTS
4 trout fillets

FOR THE MARINADE
75 ml/5 tbsp soy sauce
75 ml/5 tbsp sake or dry white wine
75 ml/5 tbsp mirin

1 Lay the trout fillets in a shallow dish in a single layer. Mix together the ingredients for the marinade and pour the marinade over the fish. Cover the dish and leave the fish to marinate in the fridge for 5–6 hours, turning occasionally.

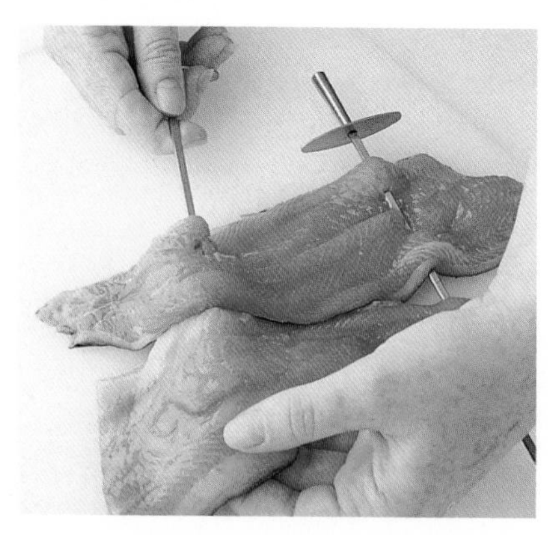

2 Thread two trout fillets neatly together on two flat metal skewers. Repeat with the remaining two fillets. You could cut the fillets in half if they are too big.

3 Grill the trout fillets under a hot grill, brushing them with the marinade several times during cooking. Grill each side of the fish until shiny and cooked all the way through. Alternatively, cook the trout on a barbecue over a high heat, keeping it at a distance of about 10 cm/4 in from the flame.

4 Slide the trout off the skewers while it is still hot. Serve the fish hot or cold with any remaining teriyaki marinade.

COOK'S TIP: To make a teriyaki barbecue sauce, heat the marinade until boiling, then reduce it until it thickens. When you grill the fish, brush it with the sauce several times. This sauce is also good with barbecued meat.

Grilled Fresh Sardines

Fresh sardines are excellent when simply grilled and served with lemon.

Serves 4–6

INGREDIENTS
1 kg/2¼ lb very fresh sardines, cleaned and with heads removed
olive oil, for brushing
salt and freshly ground black pepper
chopped fresh parsley and lemon wedges, to garnish

1 Rinse the prepared sardines in plenty of cold water. Pat them dry with kitchen paper.

2 Brush the sardines lightly with the olive oil, ensuring both sides are coated. Sprinkle each one generously with salt and freshly ground black pepper.

3 Place the sardines in one layer on the grill pan. Grill for about 3–4 minutes on one side.

4 Turn the fish and cook for 3–4 minutes more, until the skin begins to brown. Serve the sardines immediately, garnished with chopped fresh parsley and lemon wedges.

Fish Brochettes

Fresh herbs and spices make a delicious marinade for these fish kebabs.

Serves 4

INGREDIENTS
450 g/1 lb white fish fillets, such as cod, haddock, monkfish or sea bass
olive oil, for brushing
lime wedges and fresh tomato sauce, to serve

FOR THE MARINADE
½ onion, grated or very finely chopped
2 garlic cloves, crushed
30 ml/2 tbsp chopped fresh coriander
15 ml/1 tbsp chopped fresh parsley
5 ml/1 tsp ground cumin
10 ml/2 tsp paprika
good pinch of ground ginger
25 ml/1½ tbsp white wine vinegar
30 ml/2 tbsp lime juice
salt and cayenne pepper

1 First make the marinade. Blend all the ingredients and season to taste with salt and cayenne pepper.

2 Cut the fish into 1 cm/½ in cubes, discarding any skin and bones. Place in a shallow dish and add the marinade, stirring to coat thoroughly. Cover with clear film and set aside in a cool place for about 2 hours.

3 Thread the fish on to 12 small or eight larger wooden or metal kebab skewers. Place on a grill pan and brush with a little olive oil. Cook for 7–10 minutes, until the fish is cooked, turning and brushing with more oil occasionally. Serve with lime wedges and fresh tomato sauce.

Grilled Salmon Steaks with Fennel

The mild aniseed flavour of fennel goes well with all kinds of fish, but it is particularly good with salmon.

Serves 4

INGREDIENTS
juice of 1 lemon
45 ml/3 tbsp chopped fresh fennel herb, or the green fronds from the top of a fennel bulb
5 ml/1 tsp fennel seeds
45 ml/3 tbsp olive oil
4 salmon steaks of the same thickness, about 675 g/1½ lb total weight
salt and freshly ground black pepper
lemon wedges, to garnish
lightly cooked fennel, to serve

1 Combine the lemon juice, chopped fennel and fennel seeds with the olive oil in a bowl. Add the salmon steaks, turning them to coat them with the marinade. Sprinkle with salt and freshly ground black pepper. Cover and place in the fridge for 2 hours.

COOK'S TIP: Wild fennel, which grows by the sea, has a stronger flavour than the cultivated variety found in shops. Fennel also makes an excellent accompaniment to grey and red mullet.

2 Arrange the fish in one layer on a grill pan or shallow baking tray. Grill about 10 cm/4 in from the heat source for 3–4 minutes.

3 Turn the fish. Spoon on the remaining marinade and grill for 3–4 minutes on the other side, or until the edges begin to brown. Serve hot, garnished with lemon wedges and accompanied by cooked fennel.

Halibut with Fresh Tomato & Basil Salsa

Seasoning this dish well before grilling helps to bring out the delicate flavour of the fish and the fresh taste of the sauce.

Serves 4

INGREDIENTS
4 halibut fillets, about 175 g/6 oz each
45 ml/3 tbsp olive oil
fresh basil, to garnish

FOR THE SALSA
1 medium tomato, roughly chopped
¼ red onion, finely sliced
1 small jalapeño pepper, finely chopped
30 ml/2 tbsp balsamic vinegar
10 large fresh basil leaves
15 ml/1 tbsp olive oil
salt and freshly ground black pepper

1 First make the salsa. In a bowl, mix together the tomato, red onion, jalapeño pepper and balsamic vinegar. Slice the basil leaves finely. Stir into the tomato mixture with the olive oil. Season the salsa to taste. Cover and leave to marinate in a cool place for at least 3 hours.

2 Rub the halibut with olive oil and seasoning. Grill for about 4 minutes on each side depending on the thickness. Baste with olive oil as necessary. Garnish with basil and serve immediately with the salsa.

Tuna & Corn Fish Cakes

These economic little tuna fish cakes are quick to make. Either use fresh mashed potatoes, or make a storecupboard version with instant mash.

Serves 4

INGREDIENTS
300 g/11 oz/3⅔ cups cooked mashed potatoes
200 g/7 oz can tuna fish in soya oil, drained
115 g/4 oz/¾ cup canned or frozen sweetcorn
30 ml/2 tbsp chopped fresh parsley
50 g/2 oz/1 cup fresh white or brown breadcrumbs
salt and freshly ground black pepper
fresh parsley and lemon wedges, to garnish
lightly cooked green beans and carrots, to serve

1 Place the mashed potato in a bowl and stir in the tuna fish, sweetcorn and chopped parsley. Season to taste, then shape into eight patty shapes with your hands.

2 Spread out the breadcrumbs on a plate. Press the fish cakes into the breadcrumbs to coat lightly, then place on a lightly oiled baking sheet. Cook under a moderately hot grill until crisp and golden brown, turning once. Serve hot with green beans and carrots, garnished with lemon wedges and parsley.

Tuna with Oriental Dressing

A tangy dressing complements the rich flavour of grilled tuna fish.

Serves 6

INGREDIENTS
6 tuna steaks, about 900 g/2 lb total weight
cooked pasta and fresh asparagus, to serve

FOR THE DRESSING
2.5 cm/1 in fresh root ginger, peeled and finely grated
2 spring onions, thinly sliced
30 ml/2 tbsp chopped fresh chives
grated rind and juice of 1 lime or lemon
30 ml/2 tbsp dry sherry
15 ml/1 tbsp soy sauce
120 ml/4 fl oz/½ cup olive oil
salt and freshly ground black pepper

1 To make the dressing, combine the ginger, spring onions, chives, lime or lemon rind and juice, sherry and soy sauce. Whisk in the olive oil, season and set aside.

2 Season the tuna steaks with salt and freshly ground black pepper and arrange them on the rack in the grill pan. Grill for about 5 minutes on each side, until the fish flakes easily when it is tested with a fork.

3 Arrange the cooked fish steaks on a warmed serving platter or on individual plates. Spoon the dressing over the fish and serve immediately with pasta shapes of your choice and lightly steamed or roasted fresh asparagus spears.

COOK'S TIP: Do not be tempted to substitute dried ground ginger for the fresh root ginger used in this recipe. It has a completely different flavour and will not have the same impact as root ginger, with its powerful kick.

Marinated Monkfish & Mussel Skewers

This dish, with its unusual combination of flavours, is an inspired and economical way to serve monkfish.

Serves 4

INGREDIENTS
450 g/1 lb monkfish, skinned and boned
5 ml/1 tsp olive oil
30 ml/2 tbsp lemon juice
5 ml/1 tsp paprika
1 garlic clove, crushed
4 turkey rashers
8 cooked mussels
8 raw prawns, heads removed
15 ml/1 tbsp chopped fresh dill
salt and freshly ground black pepper
lemon wedges, to garnish
salad leaves and long-grain and wild rice, to serve

1 Cut the monkfish into 2.5 cm/1 in cubes and place in a shallow glass dish. Mix together the oil, lemon juice, paprika and garlic and season with freshly ground black pepper.

2 Pour the marinade over the fish and toss to coat evenly. Cover and leave in a cool place for 30 minutes.

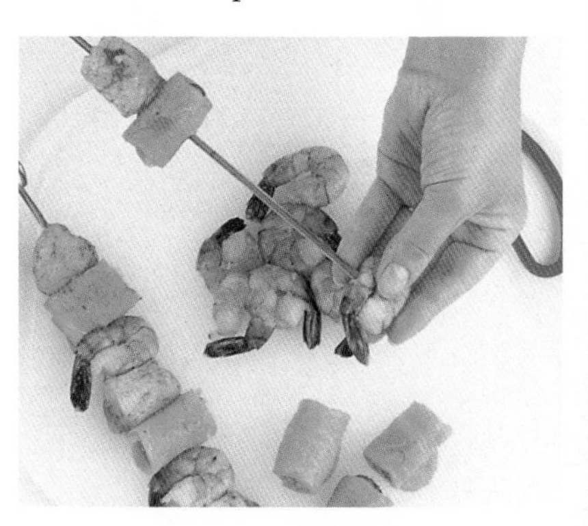

3 Cut the turkey rashers in half and wrap each strip around a mussel. Thread on to skewers, alternating with the fish cubes and raw prawns.

4 Cook the kebabs under a hot grill for 7–8 minutes, turning once and basting with the marinade.

5 Sprinkle the cooked kebabs with chopped dill and salt. Garnish with lemon wedges and serve with salad and long-grain and wild rice.

COOK'S TIP: Monkfish is ideal for kebabs, but can be expensive. Cod or hake are good alternatives.

King Prawns with Salsa Verde & Lime Wedges

A wonderfully tangy salsa accompanies these lightly grilled prawns, attractively garnished with limes.

Serves 4

INGREDIENTS
120 ml/4 fl oz/½ cup white wine
10 ml/2 tsp grated fresh root ginger
10 ml/2 tsp crushed garlic
24 raw king prawns, peeled and heads left intact
2 limes and 30 ml/2 tbsp chopped fresh coriander, to garnish

FOR THE SALSA VERDE
1 small onion, quartered
1 bunch fresh coriander
5 ml/1 tsp crushed garlic
90 ml/6 tbsp olive oil

1 Combine the white wine, ginger and garlic in a medium bowl. Add the king prawns, turning to coat them in the marinade. Cover the bowl and leave to chill for 4–6 hours.

2 Make the salsa. Chop the onion roughly in a food processor. Add the coriander and garlic and process until finely chopped. With the motor running, pour in the oil through the feeder tube of the processor. When the salsa is thick and creamy, scrape it into a serving bowl.

3 Line a grill pan with foil. Place half the prawns on the grill pan and cook for 5–6 minutes, turning them over halfway through cooking. Repeat with the remaining prawns.

4 Divide the prawns among four plates. Cut the limes in half lengthways, then into wedges. Press the long edge of each wedge into the chopped coriander. Place two wedges on each plate. Serve the prawns and lime with the salsa verde.

Chicken with Lemon & Herbs

The herbs can be changed according to what is available: for example, parsley or thyme could be used instead of tarragon and fennel.

Serves 2

INGREDIENTS
- 50 g/2 oz/4 tbsp butter
- 2 spring onions, white part only, finely chopped
- 15 ml/1 tbsp chopped fresh tarragon
- 15 ml/1 tbsp chopped fresh fennel
- juice of 1 lemon
- 4 chicken thighs
- salt and freshly ground black pepper
- lemon slices and fresh herb sprigs, to garnish
- fried potatoes, to serve

1 In a small saucepan, melt the butter, then add the spring onions, herbs, lemon juice and seasoning.

2 Brush the chicken generously with the herb mixture. Cook under a moderate grill for 10–12 minutes, basting frequently. Turn and baste again, then cook for a further 10–12 minutes or until the juices run clear.

3 Serve the chicken garnished with lemon slices and herb sprigs, and accompanied by fried potatoes and any remaining herb mixture.

Minty Yogurt Chicken

An easy, quick-to-prepare but wonderfully aromatic creamy herb marinade gives a lift to simple grilled chicken.

Serves 4

INGREDIENTS
8 chicken thighs, skinned
15 ml/1 tbsp clear honey
30 ml/2 tbsp lime or lemon juice
30 ml/2 tbsp plain yogurt
60 ml/4 tbsp chopped fresh mint
salt and freshly ground black pepper
tomato salad and boiled new potatoes, to serve

1 Slash the chicken flesh at intervals with a sharp knife and place the slashed pieces in a bowl.

2 Mix together the honey, lime or lemon juice, yogurt, seasoning and half the mint. Spoon the mixture over the chicken and leave to marinate in a cool place for 30 minutes.

3 Cook the marinated chicken under a moderately hot grill until thoroughly cooked and golden brown, turning each piece occasionally during cooking.

4 Sprinkle with the remaining mint and serve with tomato salad and new potatoes.

Grilled Spiced Chicken

This dish is delicious served with very lightly steamed green vegetables, such as mangetouts, green beans, broccoli or Chinese cabbage.

Serves 4

INGREDIENTS
5 ml/1 tsp coriander seeds
5 ml/1 tsp cumin seeds
2 limes
2 garlic cloves, crushed
60 ml/4 tbsp chopped fresh coriander
1 small green chilli, seeded and finely chopped
30 ml/2 tbsp light soy sauce
60 ml/4 tbsp sunflower oil
4 chicken breasts, skinless, boneless, about 175 g/6 oz each
steamed green vegetables, to serve

1 Crush the coriander and cumin seeds using a pestle and mortar or a herb or coffee grinder.

2 Cut the rind from the limes into thin shreds using a zester, and avoiding the pith as far as possible. Squeeze the juice from both fruits.

3 Blend the crushed coriander and cumin seeds with the lime rind and juice, crushed garlic, fresh coriander, chopped chilli, soy sauce and oil in a shallow bowl.

4 Add the prepared chicken breasts, turn each piece to coat thoroughly with the mixture, then cover the bowl with clear film and leave to marinate in the fridge for at least 4 hours. (You can leave it for up to 24 hours if you wish – the flavour will continue to improve.)

5 Remove the chicken breasts from the marinade. Cook the chicken under a pre-heated grill for about 4–6 minutes on one side. Turn the pieces over and cook for a further 4–6 minutes, or until they are cooked all the way through. Serve the spiced chicken breasts accompanied by crisp, steamed green vegetables.

Chicken Breasts Cooked in Spices & Coconut

This sweet-and-spicy chicken dish can be prepared in advance and cooked when required. Serve it with naan bread.

Serves 4

INGREDIENTS
200 g/7 oz block creamed coconut
300 ml/½ pint/1¼ cups boiling water
3 garlic cloves, chopped
2 spring onions, chopped
1 green chilli, chopped
5 cm/2 in piece fresh root ginger, chopped
5 ml/1 tsp fennel seeds
2.5 ml/½ tsp black peppercorns
seeds from 4 cardamom pods
30 ml/2 tbsp ground coriander
5 ml/1 tsp ground cumin
5 ml/1 tsp ground star anise
5 ml/1 tsp ground nutmeg
2.5 ml/½ tsp ground cloves
2.5 ml/½ tsp ground turmeric
5 ml/1 tsp salt
4 large skinless, boneless chicken breasts
onion rings and fresh coriander sprigs, to garnish

1 Break up the coconut and put it in a jug. Pour the boiling water over and leave to dissolve.

2 Place the chopped garlic, spring onions, chilli, ginger, together with all the spices and salt, in a blender or food processor. Add the dissolved coconut and process the mixture to form a smooth paste.

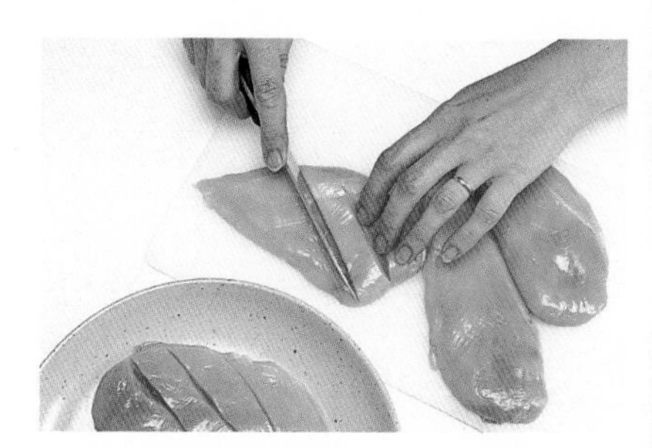

3 Make several diagonal cuts across the chicken breasts. Arrange them in one layer in a shallow dish. Spoon over half the coconut mixture and toss well to coat the chicken breasts evenly. Cover and leave to marinate in the fridge for about 30 minutes.

4 Cook the chicken under a moderate grill for 12–15 minutes, turning once, until well browned and thoroughly cooked. Heat the remaining coconut mixture gently, until it is boiling. Serve with the chicken, garnished with onion rings and sprigs of coriander.

Sirloin Steaks with Bloody Mary Sauce & Coriander

This cocktail of ingredients is just as successful as the well-known drink, but the alcohol evaporates in the cooking process, so you don't need to worry about a hangover.

Serves 4

INGREDIENTS
4 sirloin steaks, about 225 g/8 oz each

FOR THE MARINADE
30 ml/2 tbsp soy sauce
60 ml/4 tbsp balsamic vinegar
30 ml/2 tbsp olive oil

FOR THE SAUCE
1 kg/2¼ lb very ripe tomatoes, peeled and chopped
tomato purée, if required
50 g/2 oz/½ cup chopped onions
2 spring onions, chopped
5 ml/1 tsp chopped fresh coriander
5 ml/1 tsp ground cumin
5 ml/1 tsp salt
15 ml/1 tbsp lime juice
120 ml/4 fl oz/½ cup beef consommé
50 ml/2 fl oz/¼ cup vodka
15 ml/1 tbsp Worcestershire sauce

1 Lay the steaks in a shallow dish. Mix the marinade ingredients together, pour over the steaks and leave for at least 2 hours in the fridge, turning once or twice.

2 If the tomatoes do not seem quite ripe enough, add a little tomato purée. Place with all the remaining sauce ingredients in a food processor or blender and blend the mixture to a fairly smooth texture.

3 Put the blended sauce in a pan, bring to the boil and allow to simmer for about 5 minutes.

4 Remove the steaks from the marinade (discard the marinade) and grill under high heat, turning once, until cooked according to individual taste. Serve with the heated Bloody Mary sauce.

Persian Kebabs

A traditional Iranian recipe with the delicate but distinctive flavour and colour of saffron.

Serves 4

INGREDIENTS
450 g/1 lb lean lamb or beef fillet
2–3 saffron strands
1 large onion, grated
4–6 tomatoes, halved
15 ml/1 tbsp melted butter
salt and freshly ground black pepper
boiled rice, to serve

1 Cut the meat into strips about 1 cm/½ in thick and 4 cm/1½ in long, discarding any excess fat.

2 Soak the saffron in 15 ml/1 tbsp boiling water, pour into a small bowl and mix with the grated onion. Add to the meat and stir a few times so that the meat is coated thoroughly. Cover the bowl loosely with clear film and leave to marinate in the fridge for 2–3 hours.

3 Season the meat with salt and pepper and then thread on to flat skewers, aligning the strips in neat rows. Thread the tomatoes on to two separate skewers.

4 Grill the kebabs and tomatoes for 10–12 minutes, basting with butter and turning occasionally. Serve the kebabs with boiled rice.

Shish Kebab

The meat for this colourful dish may be marinated for longer – the flavour can only improve.

Serves 4

INGREDIENTS
450 g/1 lb boned leg of lamb, cubed
1 large green pepper, cut into squares
1 large yellow pepper, cut into squares
8 baby onions, halved
225 g/8 oz/3 cups button mushrooms
4 tomatoes, halved
15 ml/1 tbsp melted butter
cooked bulgur wheat, to serve

FOR THE MARINADE
45 ml/3 tbsp olive oil
juice of 1 lemon
2 garlic cloves, crushed
1 large onion, grated
15 ml/1 tbsp chopped fresh oregano
salt and freshly ground black pepper

1 Blend all the ingredients for the marinade and pour over the meat in a shallow dish. Place in the fridge for 2–3 hours.

2 Thread some skewers with lamb, pepper, onion and mushrooms, and others with tomatoes. Grill for 10–12 minutes, basting with butter and turning occasionally. Serve the kebabs with bulgur wheat.

Right: Persian Kebabs (top); Shish Kebab.

Koftas with Avocado & Melon Salsa

Tsire powder, made with ground peanuts, gives a lovely, crunchy coating to the meat on these kebabs.

Serves 4–6

INGREDIENTS
675 g/1½ lb lean minced lamb
30 ml/2 tbsp Greek-style yogurt
1 small onion, finely chopped
1 garlic clove, crushed
1.5 ml/¼ tsp chilli powder
1 egg, beaten
salt and freshly ground black pepper
fresh mint leaves, to garnish

FOR THE SALSA
1 ripe avocado
juice of 1 lime
225 g/8 oz melon, peeled, seeded and cut into small dice
4 spring onions, very finely chopped
1 red chilli, seeded and finely chopped

FOR THE TSIRE POWDER
115 g/4 oz/1 cup salted peanuts
10 ml/2 tsp ground mixed spice
5–10 ml/1–2 tsp chilli powder
salt

1 Make the salsa. Peel and stone the avocado, dice the flesh finely and toss it with the lime juice in a bowl. Add the melon, spring onions and chilli, with salt and pepper to taste. Cover the bowl closely and leave to stand for 30 minutes.

2 Make the tsire powder. Grind the peanuts to a coarse powder in a mortar, blender or food processor, then add the mixed spice, chilli powder and a little salt. Set aside.

3 Put the minced lamb in a food processor with the yogurt, onion, garlic and chilli powder. Add a little salt and pepper and process the mixture until smooth.

4 Divide the lamb mixture into 12 portions and shape each one into a sausage shape. Push a pre-soaked bamboo skewer into each kofta and press the meat on to the stick.

5 Dip each kofta in egg, then roll it in the tsire powder. Cook under a hot grill for 10 minutes, turning occasionally, until cooked. Serve with the avocado and melon salsa, garnished with mint leaves.

Rockburger Salad with Sesame Croûtons

Inside each grilled beefburger is a delicious surprise – a special layer of melting blue Roquefort cheese.

Serves 4

INGREDIENTS
900 g/2 lb lean minced beef
1 egg
1 medium onion, finely chopped
10 ml/2 tsp French mustard
2.5 ml/½ tsp celery salt
115 g/4 oz Roquefort or other blue cheese
1 large sesame-seed loaf
45 ml/3 tbsp olive oil
1 small iceberg lettuce
50 g/2 oz rocket or watercress
120 ml/4 fl oz/½ cup French dressing
4 ripe tomatoes, quartered
4 large spring onions, sliced
freshly ground black pepper

1 Place the minced beef, egg, onion, mustard, celery salt and pepper in a mixing bowl. Combine thoroughly. Divide the mixture into 16 portions, each weighing 50 g/2 oz.

2 Flatten the pieces between two sheets of polythene or waxed paper to form 13 cm/5 in rounds.

3 Place 15 g/½ oz of the cheese on eight of the thin burgers. Sandwich with the remainder and press the edges firmly. Store between pieces of polythene or waxed paper and chill until ready to cook.

4 To make the sesame croûtons, remove the crust from the bread, then cut the crust into short fingers. Moisten each of the fingers with olive oil and toast evenly under a moderate grill for 10–15 minutes.

5 Season the filled burgers according to taste, and grill for 10 minutes, turning once halfway through.

COOK'S TIP: If planning ahead, freeze the filled burgers between pieces of waxed paper and keep in the freezer for up to 8 weeks.

6 Wash the iceberg lettuce and rocket or watercress and spin dry. Toss the salad leaves with the dressing, then distribute among four large plates. Place two grilled rockburgers in the centre of each plate and the quartered tomatoes, sliced spring onions and toasted sesame croûtons around the edge.

Mexican Beefburgers

Nothing beats the flavour and quality of a home-made burger. This version, from Mexico, is seasoned with cumin and fresh coriander.

Makes 4

INGREDIENTS
4 sweetcorn cobs, husks and silks removed
50 g/2 oz/1 cup stale white breadcrumbs
90 ml/6 tbsp milk
1 small onion, finely chopped
5 ml/1 tsp ground cumin
2.5 ml/½ tsp cayenne pepper
2.5 ml/½ tsp celery salt
45 ml/3 tbsp chopped fresh coriander
900 g/2 lb lean minced beef
4 sesame-seed buns
60 ml/4 tbsp mayonnaise
8 tomato slices
½ iceberg lettuce or other leaves such as frisée or Webb's
salt and freshly ground black pepper
1 large packet corn chips, to serve

1 Bring a large saucepan of water to the boil, add a good pinch of salt and the sweetcorn cobs. Cook the sweetcorn for 15 minutes.

2 Combine the breadcrumbs, milk, onion, cumin, cayenne, celery salt and fresh coriander in a large bowl. Add the beef and mix by hand until evenly blended.

3 Divide the mixture into four equal portions and flatten into discs between sheets of clear film.

4 Grill under moderate heat for about 10 minutes for medium burgers or 15 minutes for well-done burgers, turning once during the cooking time.

5 Split and toast the sesame-seed buns. Spread the buns with mayonnaise and place a cooked burger on the base of each. Top the burgers with slices of tomato and lettuce leaves. Add salt and freshly ground black pepper to taste. Serve the burgers with corn chips and the cooked sweetcorn cobs.

Lemon Grass Pork Chops with Field Mushrooms

The pork is infused with fabulous Far Eastern flavours both from the marinade and from the warm dressing served with it.

Serves 4

INGREDIENTS
4 pork chops
4 large field mushrooms
45 ml/3 tbsp vegetable oil
4 red chillies, seeded and finely sliced
45 ml/3 tbsp fish sauce
90 ml/6 tbsp lime juice
4 shallots, chopped
5 ml/1 tsp ground rice, roasted
30 ml/2 tbsp spring onions, chopped
fresh coriander leaves and shredded spring onions, to garnish

FOR THE MARINADE
2 garlic cloves, chopped
15 ml/1 tbsp sugar
15 ml/1 tbsp fish sauce
30 ml/2 tbsp soy sauce
15 ml/1 tbsp sesame oil
15 ml/1 tbsp whisky or dry sherry
2 lemon grass stalks, finely chopped
2 spring onions, chopped

1 To make the marinade, put all the marinade ingredients into a bowl and mix well together.

2 In a shallow bowl, pour the marinade over the pork chops and leave in a cool place for 1–2 hours.

3 Place the mushrooms and marinated pork chops on a grill pan and brush with 15 ml/1 tbsp of the oil. Grill the chops for 5–7 minutes on each side and the mushrooms for about 2 minutes. Brush both with the marinade while grilling.

4 Meanwhile heat the rest of the oil in a small frying pan, then remove from the heat and mix in the remaining ingredients except for the garnish. Put the pork chops and mushrooms on a serving plate and spoon over the sauce. Garnish with coriander and shredded spring onion.

Red Bean & Mushroom Burgers

Vegetarians, vegans and even meat-eaters can all enjoy these healthy, low fat veggie burgers which work equally well grilled or barbecued.

Serves 4

INGREDIENTS
15 ml/1 tbsp olive oil
1 small onion, finely chopped
1 garlic clove, crushed
5 ml/1 tsp ground cumin
5 ml/1 tsp ground coriander
2.5 ml/½ tsp ground turmeric
115 g/4 oz/1½ cups finely chopped mushrooms
400 g/14 oz can red kidney beans
30 ml/2 tbsp chopped fresh coriander
wholemeal flour
olive oil, for brushing
salt and freshly ground black pepper
salad and pitta bread, to serve

1 Heat the oil and fry the onion and garlic over moderate heat until softened. Add the spices and cook for a further minute, stirring continuously.

2 Add the mushrooms and cook, stirring, until softened and dry. Remove from the heat.

3 Drain the kidney beans thoroughly, rinse in cold water and them mash them with a fork.

4 Stir the beans into the pan, with the fresh coriander, mixing thoroughly. Season well with salt and freshly ground black pepper.

5 Using floured hands, form the mixture into four flat burger shapes. If the mixture is too sticky to handle, mix in a little flour.

COOK'S TIP: These burgers are not quite as firm as meat burgers, so handle them gently during cooking.

6 Brush both sides of the burgers with oil. Place under a hot grill and cook for 8–10 minutes, turning halfway through.

7 When the burgers are cooked and golden brown on both sides, serve them with pitta bread and crisp green salad leaves.

Pitta Pizzas

Pitta breads make very good bases for quick, thin and crispy pizzas, and they are easy to eat with your hands too: the perfect speedy snack.

Serves 4

INGREDIENTS
4 pitta breads, preferably wholemeal
1 small jar of pasta sauce
225 g/8 oz Mozzarella cheese, sliced or grated
dried oregano or thyme, to sprinkle
salt and freshly ground black pepper

FOR THE TOPPINGS
1 small red onion, thinly sliced and lightly fried
mushrooms, sliced and fried
200 g/7 oz can sweetcorn, drained
jalapeño chillies, seeded and sliced
black or green olives, stoned and sliced
capers, drained

1 Prepare two or three toppings of your choice for the pizzas.

2 Preheat the grill and lightly toast the pitta breads on each side.

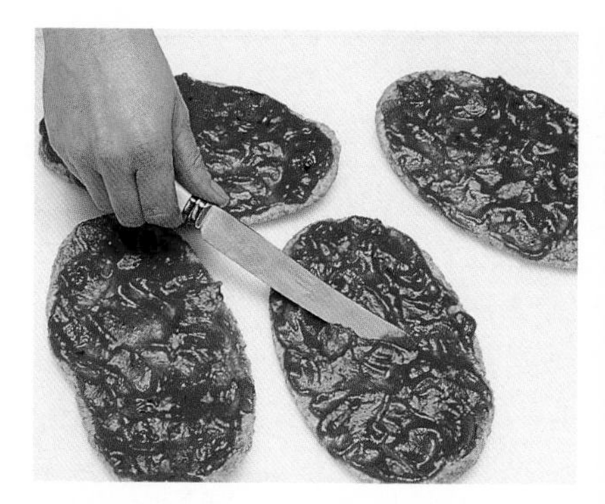

3 Spread pasta sauce on each pitta, right to the edge. This prevents the edges of the pitta from burning.

4 Arrange cheese slices or grated cheese on top of each pitta and sprinkle with herbs and seasoning.

5 Add the toppings of your choice and then grill the pizzas for about 5–8 minutes, until they are golden brown and bubbling. Serve the pitta pizzas immediately.

Leek & Cheese Sausages

These tasty sausages are ideal for vegetarians and, as they freeze very well, are useful to have as a standby.

Makes 8

INGREDIENTS
150 g/5 oz/2½ cups fresh breadcrumbs
150 g/5 oz/generous 1 cup grated Caerphilly cheese
1 small leek, very finely chopped
15 ml/1 tbsp chopped fresh parsley
leaves from 1 thyme sprig, chopped
2 eggs
7.5 ml/1½ tsp English mustard powder
about 45 ml/3 tbsp milk
plain flour, for coating
15 ml/1 tbsp oil
15 g/½ oz/1 tbsp melted butter
salt and freshly ground black pepper
salad, to serve

1 Mix the breadcrumbs, grated cheese, chopped leek, parsley, thyme, salt and pepper. Whisk the eggs with the mustard powder and set aside 30 ml/2 tbsp for later. Stir the remainder into the cheese mixture with enough milk to bind.

2 Divide the cheese mixture into eight equal portions and form into sausage shapes.

3 Dip the sausages in the reserved egg to coat. Season the flour, then roll the sausages in it to give a light, even coating. Chill for about 30 minutes, until firm.

4 Oil the grill rack. Mix the remaining oil and melted butter together and brush over the sausages. Grill the sausages for 5–10 minutes, turning carefully occasionally, until golden brown all over. Serve hot or cold with salad.

Brie Parcels with Almonds

A sophisticated, light main course, delicious served with crusty bread.

Serves 4

INGREDIENTS
4 large vine leaves, preserved in brine
200 g/7 oz piece Brie
30 ml/2 tbsp chopped fresh chives
30 ml/2 tbsp ground almonds
5 ml/1 tsp crushed black peppercorns
15 ml/1 tbsp olive oil, plus extra for brushing
flaked almonds

1 Rinse the vine leaves thoroughly in cold water and dry them well. Spread the leaves out on a board.

2 Cut the Brie into four equal chunks and place each chunk in the centre of a vine leaf.

3 Mix together the chives, ground almonds, crushed black peppercorns and oil, then place a spoonful on top of each piece of cheese. Sprinkle with flaked almonds.

4 Fold the vine leaves over, to enclose the cheese completely. Turn over, so the ends are underneath. Brush with oil and cook under a hot grill for 3–4 minutes, until the cheese is hot and melting. Serve immediately.

COOK'S TIP: This dish also makes an elegant vegetarian starter.

Mushrooms with Leeks & Stilton

Upturned mushroom caps make perfect containers for this mouth-watering leek and Stilton filling.

Serves 2–3

INGREDIENTS
1 leek, thinly sliced
6 flat mushrooms
2 garlic cloves, crushed
30 ml/2 tbsp chopped fresh parsley
115 g/4 oz/½ cup butter, softened
115 g/4 oz Stilton cheese
freshly ground black pepper
frisée and tomato halves, to garnish

1 Put the leek slices in a small pan with a little water. Cover and cook for about 5 minutes, until tender. Drain, refresh under cold water and then drain again.

2 Remove the stalks from the mushrooms and set them aside. Put the mushroom caps, hollows uppermost, on an oiled baking sheet.

3 Put the mushroom stalks, garlic and parsley in a food processor or blender. Process for 1 minute. Tip into a bowl, add the leek and butter and season with pepper to taste.

4 Crumble the Stilton into the mushroom mixture and mix well. Divide among the mushroom caps and grill for 6–7 minutes, until bubbling. Serve garnished with frisée and halved tomatoes.

Vegetable Kebabs with Mustard & Honey

A colourful mixture of vegetables and tofu, skewered, glazed and grilled until tender. Soak bamboo skewers in cold water first to prevent burning.

Serves 4

INGREDIENTS
1 yellow pepper
2 small courgettes
225 g/8 oz piece firm tofu
8 cherry tomatoes
8 button mushrooms
15 ml/1 tbsp wholegrain mustard
15 ml/1 tbsp clear honey
30 ml/2 tbsp olive oil
salt and freshly ground black pepper

TO SERVE
4 portions cooked mixed long-grain and wild rice
lime segments
flat leaf parsley

1 Cut the yellow pepper in half and remove the seeds. Cut each half into quarters and cut each quarter in half again.

2 Top and tail the courgettes and peel them decoratively, if you like. Cut each courgette into eight chunks. Cut the tofu into pieces of a similar size.

3 Thread a mixture of the pepper pieces, courgette chunks, tofu, cherry tomatoes and mushrooms on to four metal or bamboo skewers.

4 Whisk the mustard, honey and olive oil in a small bowl. Add salt and pepper to taste.

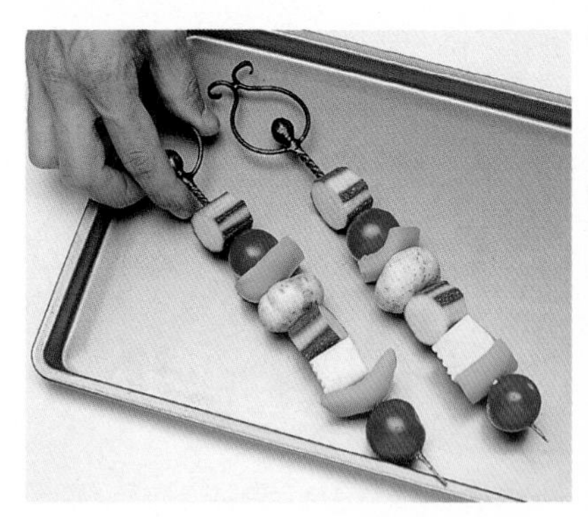

5 Put the kebabs on to a baking sheet. Brush with the mustard and honey glaze. Cook under the grill for 8 minutes, turning once or twice during cooking. Serve with a mixture of long-grain and wild rice, garnished with lime segments and parsley.

Grilled Corn with Ginger Hazelnut Butter

Take care to cook the corn slowly, so as not to dry it out.

Serves 4

INGREDIENTS
15 ml/1 tbsp olive oil
45 ml/3 tbsp finely chopped hazelnuts
2.5 cm/1 in piece fresh root ginger, finely chopped
75 g/3 oz/6 tbsp butter
4 sweetcorn cobs
salt and freshly ground black pepper

1 Heat the oil in a small pan and gently fry the hazelnuts, stirring, until they are golden brown.

2 Remove the hazelnuts from the heat, cool slightly, and then stir in the ginger. Mix in the butter, with salt and pepper to taste.

3 Remove the husks and silks from the sweetcorn cobs and grill them under a gentle heat, for 20–25 minutes. Turn the cobs frequently throughout the cooking time.

4 When the cobs are tender and golden brown on all sides, drizzle with the ginger hazelnut butter and serve immediately.

Grilled Peppers with Olives

This colourful salad captures the sunshine of the Mediterranean.

Serves 6

INGREDIENTS
4 large peppers, red or yellow or a combination of both
30 ml/2 tbsp capers in salt, vinegar or brine, rinsed
18–20 black or green olives

FOR THE DRESSING
90 ml/6 tbsp extra-virgin olive oil
2 garlic cloves, crushed
30 ml/2 tbsp balsamic or wine vinegar
salt and freshly ground black pepper

1 Place the peppers under a hot grill, and turn occasionally until they are black and blistered on all sides. Remove from the heat and place in a paper bag. Leave for 5 minutes.

2 Peel the peppers, cut into strips and discard the seeds. Arrange in a serving dish and top evenly with the capers and olives.

3 For the dressing, mix the oil and garlic in a bowl. Add the vinegar and seasoning. Stir into the salad at least 30 minutes before serving.

Pineapple Wedges with Rum Butter Glaze

Fresh pineapple is even more full of flavour when grilled; this spiced rum glaze makes it into a very special dessert.

Serves 4

INGREDIENTS
1 medium pineapple
30 ml/2 tbsp dark muscovado sugar
5 ml/1 tsp ground ginger
60 ml/4 tbsp melted butter
30 ml/2 tbsp dark rum

1 With a large, sharp knife, cut the pineapple lengthways into four wedges. Cut out and discard the hard core from the centre.

2 Cut between the flesh and skin to release the flesh but leave the skin. Slice the flesh across, into chunks.

COOK'S TIP: For an easier version, simply cut off the skin, slice the whole pineapple into thick slices and cook as above.

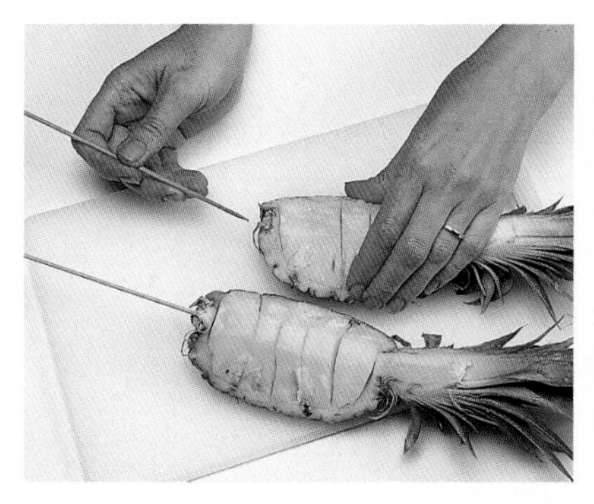

3 Push a bamboo skewer lengthways through each wedge and into the stalk, to hold the chunks in place.

4 Mix together the sugar, ginger, melted butter and rum and brush over the pineapple.

5 Cook the pineapple wedges under a hot grill for 3–4 minutes. Pour the remaining rum butter glaze over the top and serve immediately.

Nectarines with Marzipan & Mascarpone

A luscious dessert that no one can resist – dieters may like to use low fat soft cheese instead of Mascarpone.

Serves 4

INGREDIENTS
4 firm, ripe nectarines or peaches
75 g/3 oz marzipan
75 g/3 oz/5 tbsp Mascarpone
3 macaroon biscuits, crushed

1 Cut the nectarines or peaches in half, removing the stones carefully with your fingers.

2 Cut the marzipan into eight pieces and press one piece into the stone cavity of each nectarine or peach half.

3 Spoon the Mascarpone on top. Sprinkle the crushed macaroons over the Mascarpone.

4 Place the half-fruits under a hot grill for 3–5 minutes, until they are hot and the Mascarpone starts to melt.

COOK'S TIP: Either peaches or nectarines can be used for this recipe. If the stone does not pull out easily when you halve the fruit, use a small, sharp knife to cut around it.

Fruit Kebabs with Chocolate & Marshmallow Fondue

Children love these colourful and unusual treats – and with some supervision they can help to make them.

Serves 4

INGREDIENTS
2 bananas
2 kiwi fruit
12 strawberries
15 ml/1 tbsp melted butter
15 ml/1 tbsp lemon juice
5 ml/1 tsp ground cinnamon

FOR THE FONDUE
225 g/8 oz plain chocolate
120 ml/4 fl oz/½ cup single cream
8 marshmallows
2.5 ml/½ tsp vanilla essence

1 Peel the bananas and cut each into six thick chunks. Peel the kiwi fruit thinly and quarter them.

2 Thread the pieces of banana, kiwi fruit and the strawberries on to four wooden or bamboo skewers, mixing the different fruits.

3 Mix together the butter, lemon juice and cinnamon and brush the mixture over the fruits.

4 For the fondue, place the chocolate, cream and marshmallows in a small pan and heat gently, without boiling, stirring until the mixture has melted and is smooth.

5 Cook the kebabs under the grill for 2–3 minutes, turning once, or until golden. Stir the vanilla into the fondue and serve with the kebabs.

Hot Fruit with Maple Butter

Fruit salads don't always have to be cold, as this heavenly combination of hot tropical fruits proves.

Serves 4

INGREDIENTS
1 large pawpaw
1 large mango
1 small pineapple
2 bananas
115 g/4 oz/½ cup unsalted butter
60 ml/4 tbsp pure maple syrup
ground cinnamon, for sprinkling

1 Prepare the fruit just before grilling so it won't discolour. Halve the pawpaw and scoop out the seeds. Cut the flesh into thick slices, then peel away the skin.

2 Peel the mango and cut the flesh into large pieces, discarding the central stone and skin.

3 Peel and core the pineapple and slice the flesh across into thin wedges. Peel the bananas and cut them in half lengthways.

4 Cut the butter into small dice and place in a food processor with the maple syrup. Process until the mixture is smooth and creamy.

5 Place the pawpaw, mango, pineapple and banana on a grill rack and brush with the maple syrup butter. Grill the fruit under medium heat for about 10 minutes, until just tender, turning occasionally and brushing with the butter.

6 Arrange the fruit on a warmed serving platter and dot with the remaining butter. Sprinkle over a little cinnamon and serve piping hot.

COOK'S TIP: When buying maple syrup, check the label to make sure that it is 100% pure as imitations taste little like the real thing.

Index

First published in 1999 by Lorenz Books

Lorenz Books is an imprint of Anness Publishing Limited, Hermes House
88-89 Blackfriars Road, London SE1 8HA

This edition distributed in Canada by Raincoast Books, 8680 Cambie Street,
Vancouver, British Columbia, V6P 6M9

ISBN 0-7548-0123-3

A CIP catalogue record for this book is available from the British Library.

Publisher: Joanna Lorenz
Editor: Valerie Ferguson
Series Designer: Bobbie Colgate Stone
Designer: Andrew Heath
Production Controller: Joanna King

Recipes contributed by: Catherine Atkinson, Janet Brinkworth, Carla Capalbo, Kit Chan, Roz Denny, Matthew Drennan, Christine France, Shirley Gill, Rebekah Hassan, Soheila Kimberley, Masaki Ko, Gilly Love, Lesley Mackley, Norma Miller, Katherine Richmond, Liz Trigg, Hilaire Walden, Steven Wheeler.

Photography: William Adams-Lingwood, Karl Adamson, Edward Allwright, Steve Baxter, James Duncan, John Freeman,Michelle Garrett, Amanda Heywood, Don Last, Patrick McLeavey, Michael Michaels, Thomas Odulate, Juliet Piddington.

1 3 5 7 9 10 8 6 4 2

Notes:
For all recipes, quantities are given in both metric and imperial measures and, where appropriate, measures are also given in standard cups and spoons. Follow one set, but not a mixture, because they are not interchangeable.

Standard spoon and cup measures are level.

1 tsp = 5 ml 1 tbsp =15 ml

1 cup = 250 ml/8 fl oz

Australian standard tablespoons are 20 ml. Australian readers should use 3 tsp in place of 1 tbsp for measuring small quantities of gelatine, cornflour, salt, etc.

Medium eggs are used unless otherwise stated.

Printed in Singapore